AF131441

BOOK ANALYSIS

By Benjamin Taylor

The Jungle Book
BY RUDYARD KIPLING

RUDYARD KIPLING

ENGLISH NOVELIST, POET AND SHORT STORY WRITER

- **Born in Bombay (India) in 1865.**
- **Died in London in 1936.**
- **Notable works:**
  - *Captains Courageous* (1897), novel
  - *Kim* (1901), novel
  - *Just So Stories* (1902), story collection

Rudyard Kipling is considered one of the most eminent English writers of his generation and is remembered for his writings on the British Empire, India and his children's stories. Although his infamous celebration of European imperialism means that he is sometimes regarded as antiquated and problematic in the context of increasingly socially liberal Western societies, his novels, stories and poetry are highly regarded for their expertise, ingenuity and vibrancy. He was born in Bombay (now Mumbai) in 1965 to English parents and, after being educated in England, returned to India to work as a journalist. It was here that he began publishing his poetry and short stories, and he returned to England in 1889 to fanfare about the quality and popularity of his writing. In England Kipling found himself increasingly well-regarded as a writer and embarked on a prolific career that included a huge number of short stories and poetry collections, as well as four novels. In 1907, he became the first English person to win the coveted Nobel Prize for Literature, and he continued to write right up to his death in 1936, at the age of 70.

THE JUNGLE BOOK

TALES FROM THE ANIMAL KINGDOM

- **Genre:** short story collection
- **Reference edition:** Kipling, R. (1994) *The Jungle Book*. London: Penguin Books.
- **1ˢᵗ edition:** 1894
- **Themes:** animals, the outsider, identity, children's stories, colonialism, British Empire, India, superstition, nature

Thanks in part to the notable popular film and musical adaptations that have appeared since it was first published, *The Jungle Book* has become one of the most famous collections of children's stories ever written. Many of the stories within the collection are set in an unnamed jungle in India and concern the lives of various personified animals within their various animal societies. The book deals with such themes as law and order, identity and outsiderdom, and Mowgli's struggles with his identity and abandonment are often seen as connected to Kipling's relationship with his own parents, who sent him to England at the age of five to live with foster parents. Due to Kipling's colonial allegiances, the stories have sometimes been called into question as culturally problematic Anglo-Indian Imperial texts with skewed presentations of 'native' populations. The work has nonetheless been highly successful in Britain and overseas and remains a staple of national children's literature to this day.

SUMMARY

MOWGLI'S BROTHERS

One night in the Jungle, a mother and father wolf save a human child from the clutches of Shere Khan, the tiger. Though he protests, claiming it as his kill, the wolves refuse and adopt the child, who they name Mowgli. They then take him to the Jungle Council of wolves, where the pack judge whether their decision coincides with the Law of the Jungle. At the Council the wolves are wary and angry about the fact that Mowgli is a man. Shere Khan skulks, calling out to be given back his kill, but Akela, the old leader of the wolves, ignores him. Mowgli's entry into the pack is backed by Baloo the bear, who teaches the young wolves about the Law of the Jungle, and Bagheera the panther, who offers them a dead bull as compensation.

Ten years later, Mowgli has learnt the ways of the Jungle, with Baloo and Bagheera as his guides. All of them are wary of Shere Khan. He has been seen regularly in the Jungle, gaining followers amongst the younger wolves, and Bagheera is worried that once Akela becomes too old to lead the pack, Shere Khan will use the opportunity to sway them against Mowgli – who is an outsider because of his species – and finally claim his prize. In preparation for this, Bagheera gets Mowgli to go to the nearby human village and steal fire – which all animals are afraid of. The night comes when Akela's leadership is challenged by the pack. At the Jungle Council meeting, Shere Khan convinces many of the wolves, despite protestations from Bagheera and Akela, that Mowgli should be killed. Having followed Bagheera's advice, however, Mowgli brings out the fire and beats the tiger and many of the escaping wolves with a burning stick – and vows to return one day wearing Shere Khan's pelt. He weeps, however, when he realises that he must now leave the Jungle and return to the human world.

KAA'S HUNTING

The story jumps to a time before this happened, when Baloo and Bagheera were teaching Mowgli the ways of the forest, and the different languages with which one could befriend different animals. Mowgli had been speaking to the monkeys, who are derided in the forest for having no laws, lying and being wild and chaotic. One day they steal Mowgli from his teachers, taking him all the way across the forest to an ancient Indian ruin which they call home. Baloo and Bagheera cannot keep up and go to Kaa the snake to ask for help. The three go to the ruined city and fight hundreds of the monkeys, getting seriously hurt in the process. They manage to save Mowgli, however, and leave Kaa to hunt the monkeys, who are terrified of him.

TIGER! TIGER!

Back in the present, Mowgli returns to the human village near the Jungle. They instantly recognise him as the child taken ten years earlier, and he is returned to his birth mother, Messua. Mowgli finds adapting to life in the human world hard and is just as much an outsider as a result of his upbringing as he was in the Jungle for his humanity. He meets regularly with one of his wolf brothers, who tells him of the movements of Shere Khan. Eventually, Mowgli is given duties by the humans to shepherd the cows and the bulls. One day, his wolf brother tells him of Shere Khan's whereabouts, and his relative weakness and Mowgli manages to trap him in a ravine and trample him to death with the herds of bulls. Mowgli skins the tiger, but in the process frightens the humans, who cast him out of the village as an evil spirit.

Mowgli returns to the Jungle, showing the pack and his wolf mother the hide of Shere Khan, and vows to hunt alone with his wolf brothers. It is revealed that later in life Mowgli will leave the Jungle and marry but not in this story.

THE WHITE SEAL

In a completely different story, a pure white seal named Kotick is born on the island of Novastoshna. He grows up on the island joyfully with his mother and his father. One day, humans arrive, and he discovers that they annually kill many hundreds of the seals for their hides. They leave Kotick alone, however, because of his whiteness, which they are superstitious about. Kotick then goes on a journey to try and find a beach where humans do not go, and the seal herd can live in peace. He is told to find the Sea

Cows, who it is claimed will lead Kotick to an island without humans. Kotick scours the Pacific Ocean for the Sea Cows, going to many islands and finding humans on each one.

Finally, when all hope seems lost, he finds a herd of Sea Cows, who lead him to a beautiful deserted island perfect for the seals. Kotick returns immediately to Novastoshna and convinces them to join him on the island.

RIKKI-TIKKI-TAVI

One day a family find a half-drowned mongoose named Rikki-tikki and decide to keep him in order to protect their young son, Teddy, from snakes.

In the garden one day, Rikki-tikki comes across a bird named Darzee and his wife grieving the loss of one of their young, killed and eaten by a cobra named Nag. Nag emerges, confronting Rikki-tikki, and he is almost killed by Nag's wife, Nagaina, but is saved thanks to the warning of Darzee. When he goes back to the house, the mongoose manages to kill a snake threatening Teddy, impressing the family. Later that night, Rikki-tikki finds out that the cobras are planning to enter through the bathroom to kill the family. Rikki-tikki waits in the bathroom and kills Nag while he sleeps.

Rikki-tikki must now concentrate on the grieving Nagaina, who enters the house and corners the family at the breakfast table, hoping to kill Teddy in vengeance. Rikki-tikki, however, has been busy destroying her cobra eggs, and lures her out with the threat of destroying the last one. He then follows her into her hole and kills her.

TOOMAI OF THE ELEPHANTS

This is the story of Toomai, a young Indian boy whose family owns an old fighting elephant named Kala Nag. His father is among a group of elephant handlers who help capture wild elephants for the British army, led by Peterson Sahib, a white man who is said to know more about elephants than any man alive. One night at camp, Toomai notices something strange about Kala Nag, who refuses to sleep. Eventually the elephant slips away, and Toomai follows him and is lifted onto his back. They go to a clearing in which many dozens of elephants have gathered, and all appear to talk amongst each other in their elephant language, to Toomai's astonishment. He then witnesses something no man has ever seen – the dance of the elephants – as they go up onto their hind legs and stamp down on the floor repeatedly. They return to camp in the morning and Toomai is treated as a hero for what he has witnessed.

HER MAJESTY'S SERVANTS

This story tells of the events in a vast military camp on the night before the Amir of Afghanistan's visit to the Viceroy of India. Told from the perspective of a human who seems to understand animal language, it covers an argument between several different war animals, including camels, elephants and horses, about cowardice in war, their relationships to the people who exploit them and why they do what humans tell them to do.

CHARACTERS

MOWGLI

Mowgli is the central character of *The Jungle Book*, saved as a child by wolves from the jaws of Shere Khan, the tiger who makes it his life's mission to kill him. As such, Mowgli grows up amongst the wolves and the other animals of the Jungle, learning their customs and way of life rather than that of his native people: "he was only a boy – though he would have called himself a wolf if he had been able to speak in any human tongue" (p. 16). Despite the nature of his upbringing, however, Mowgli is ostracised by some of the animals of the Jungle who do not understand him as a result of his essential humanity and intelligence: "He is wise and well-taught, and above all has the eyes that make the jungle-people afraid" (p. 44).

Though Mowgli is much maligned because of what makes him different, he nevertheless has allies within the Jungle and has deep and meaningful relationships with many of the animals, including his adopted wolf family, and his teachers Baloo and Bagheera, who guide him through life in the Jungle and teach him the ways of the beasts. When Mowgli returns to the human world, he finds himself just as ostracised as before and indeed the combination of his natural human intelligence and his upbringing seems to make him superior in both the human and the animal world. He is as such representative of a species hybridity, not belonging wholly to either world, and the end of the story seems to reflect this, as it is revealed that he returns to the human world as a man to marry, apparently shifting between the two worlds at will.

BAGHEERA

Bagheera is a black panther, and much feared and respected in the Jungle. He is described as "inky-black all over, but with the panther markings showing up in certain lights like the pattern of watered silk" (p. 12), and is seemingly ever-present during Mowgli's formative years, guiding and advising him throughout the story. Bagheera notably saves Mowgli at the Council meeting by offering a bull in exchange for his membership to the pack. It is later revealed that Bagheera does this because he is familiar with the ways of humans, and therefore sympathetic to Mowgli, having lived for much of his life in captivity: "*I*, Bagheera – carry that mark, the mark of the collar" (p. 18). Bagheera loves Mowgli deeply and acts as a father figure to the boy, using his knowledge of both the human world and the animal kingdom to do right by him. Bagheera is proud, ferocious and above all respected throughout the Jungle: "Everybody knew Bagheera, and nobody cared to cross his path; for he was as cunning as Tabaqui, as bold as the wild buffalo and as reckless as the wounded elephant" (p. 12).

BALOO

Baloo is a bear, known throughout the Jungle as wise, kind and gentle. He is described early on in the story as "the sleepy brown bear who teaches wolf-cubs the Law of the Jungle: old Baloo who can come and go as he pleases because he eats only nuts and roots and honey" (p. 12). He is welcome in and amongst the wolf pack and uses his knowledge of the Law of the Jungle to vouch for

Mowgli at the beginning of the story, as he believes it to be lawful that he should be admitted into the pack. Along with Bagheera, Baloo acts as a father figure to Mowgli, and the two share a deep relationship. The extent of his love for Mowgli is clear when the child is captured by the monkeys and Baloo is clearly upset and wholly blames himself for the situation. During the fight to save him, however, he truly shows the duality of his nature, the gentle teacher and friend fighting savagely and killing many of the monkeys.

SHERE KHAN

Shere Khan is the great tiger who acts as the story's antagonist to Mowgli's protagonist. Since Mowgli was first separated from his parents, Shere Khan has claimed ownership over Mowgli's life and makes it his mission to have Mowgli thrown out of the pack in order to kill him. We are told by Mother Wolf that "he has been lame in one foot from birth. That is why he has only killed cattle" (p. 3). He is much maligned by the older, traditional, law-abiding animals of the Jungle due to his penchant for killing and eating cattle and even humans – an act which in the story frames him as malicious and twisted. The tiger is often portrayed as a figure of weakness and cowardice, relying on his ability to control and influence others, including the hyena Tabaqui and his lackeys amongst the younger wolves, to get what he wants. He is humiliated by Mowgli during the Council meeting when the boy takes advantage of the tiger's desperate fear of fire and beats him. Shere Khan later meets his end through Mowgli, who with the help of Akela directs a herd of stampeding bulls over him.

ANALYSIS

HUMANS VS ANIMALS

Much of *The Jungle Book* concerns the intricacies of and variations between the human and animal worlds – which are portrayed as two very different societies. The exploration of these two contrasting worlds which lie right next to each other is of course represented in the character of Mowgli, who belongs to each and to neither at the same time. It is evident throughout the stories that Kipling's sympathies clearly lie with the animals, many of whom are portrayed as brave, proud, logical and above all highly lawful throughout. Indeed, Kipling seems awed by the power and ingenuity of the natural world: for example, Kaa the snake is described as "everything that the monkeys feared in the Jungle, for none of them knew the limits of his power" (p. 59). This can also be seen in the mongoose Rikki-tikki, who is lauded by the father of the human family he lives with as "a providence" (p. 139) but who is bemused by the praise, having done exactly what he feels he is meant to do by killing the snake.

Humans, on the other hand, are often portrayed in *The Jungle Book* as cruel, brutal and superstitious – "the weakest and most defenceless of all living things" (p. 4). Many of the animals who have had dealings with humans seem to share this view of humanity. For example, Akela had "once been beaten and left for dead; so he knew the manners and customs of men" (pp. 10-11). Kotick the seal also sees this during his first experience with men – who club many of his young friends to death for their pelts. Just as, in the human world, many of the animals of the Jungle are generally feared, so too are the animals wary of the threat, of "the arrival of white men on elephants, with guns, and hundreds of brown men with gongs and rockets and torches. Then everybody in the Jungle suffers" (pp. 4-5). It is likely that we get such a negative view of human society due to the fact that many of the stories are told from the perspective of animals – who fear what they do not understand, just as humans do. Kipling does, however, shine a light on the way that animals are abused and exploited by humans, including

Bagheera, who was kept in captivity for much of his life, the elephant Kala Nag, who was forced into slavery as a fighting elephant for his entire life, and the war animals conversing in the story *Her Majesty's Servants*, who are forced into wars at the behest of the British Empire.

THE LAW OF THE JUNGLE

Another curious contrast between the human and animal worlds is an ideological one. What runs through many of the animal worlds is a sense of societal structure defined by 'The Law of the Jungle', or in the case of *The White Seal* 'The Law of the Beach' – a set of rules by which animals must live if they are to be accepted. These laws are particularly prominent in the stories concerning Mowgli and his battle with Shere Khan, as his very existence in the Jungle is reliant on Baloo's understanding of the Laws of the Jungle. In contrast, human society is often portrayed as highly superstitious. This can be seen, for example, when Mowgli returns to the village of his birth. He laughs at Buldeo – the chief hunter – for the wildly mystical and false stories he tells about the animals in the Jungle.

According to him, Shere Khan is "a ghost-tiger, and his body was inhabited by the ghost of a wicked old money-lender" (p. 77). The man who Kotick meets similarly believes him to be a misguided spirit: "there has never been a white seal since – since I was born. Perhaps it is old Zaharrof's ghost". (p. 110).

In presenting the mysticism at the heart of human society in this way, Kipling subverts the idea of civilisation, which is typically associated with mankind. Instead, in these stories, it is largely the animals who are just, logical and ruled by a set of laws "which never orders anything without a reason" (p. 4). The humans in *The Jungle Book* fear what they do not understand and as such attempt to place their own meaning on such situations. This can be seen the villagers' distrust of Mowgli, who they force out when he kills and skins Shere Khan: "Sorcerer! Wolf's brat! Jungle demon! Go away! Get hence quickly or the priest will turn thee into a wolf again." (p. 91). Kipling seems to attempt to rationalise these fears by imagining a personified human society within the animal kingdom.

OUTSIDERDOM

The central theme of *The Jungle Book* – particularly those stories concerning Mowgli – is that of outsiderdom and the way that he is ostracised from society as a result of his abnormality. Due to the nature of his upbringing, Mowgli is in fact presented almost as being of hybrid species – somewhere in between animal and human. It is perhaps a contributing factor to *The Jungle Book*'s lasting legacy that there seems to be a cultural fascination with this phenomenon, and symbols of popular culture like the werewolf, centaurs and mermaids stand as a testament to it. Mowgli is turned out of both the human and the animal worlds as a result of his human intelligence and his animal instincts. Bagheera claims that "the others hate thee because their eyes cannot meet thine – because though art wise – because though hast pulled out thorns from their feet – because though art a man" (p. 19). Conversely, in the human village, Mowgli thinks "now I am silly and dumb as a man would be with us in the Jungle" (p. 73) when he realises that he is unable to learn the language. He is then thrown out of the village for his animalistic tendencies, and he exclaims "Again? Last time it was because I was a man. This time it is because I am a wolf" (p. 92). As such, Mowgli lives somewhere in between these two societies.

Outsiderdom is indeed a running theme in Kipling's work. It may be useful, for example, to compare *The Jungle Book* to the titular character of Kipling's famous novel *Kim,* who finds himself similarly out of place in society having been born to Irish parents but raised an orphan on the streets of Lahore.

FURTHER REFLECTION

SOME QUESTIONS TO THINK ABOUT...

- What signs of British colonialism can be seen in *The Jungle Book*? Should Kipling's treatment of race relations be seen as problematic?
- Do you think that the portrayal of humans in the book is accurate? How else might an animal see humans in the present day?
- Compare Mowgli to Kimball O'Hara – the main character of Kipling's other famous work *Kim*. Are there any similarities/differences between them?
- The novel contains long, detailed passages describing the natural beauty of the Indian Jungle. Do you think this reflects Kipling's own love of the country?
- Compare *The Jungle Book* to any adaptations you have seen. Do you think it works better as a book or a film? What would you change from the book in a film adaptation?

- What do you think of the way that Kipling personifies the animals in the book? Is he just projecting human personalities onto animals?
- What makes the character of Mowgli who he is? Is he shaped more by his upbringing or his heritage? How does Mowgli's identity shift throughout the novel?
- Can you see any similarities between Mowgli and Kipling's own life?
- Why do you think that the story of Mowgli and Shere Khan is more popular than the other stories in the book?

We want to hear from you!
Leave a comment on your online library
and share your favourite books on social media!

FURTHER READING

REFERENCE EDITION

- Kipling, R. (1994) *The Jungle Book*. London: Penguin Books.

ADAPTATIONS

- *The Jungle Book*. (2016) [Film]. Jon Favreau. Dir. USA: Walt Disney Pictures.
- *The Jungle Book*. (1967) [Film]. Wolfgang Reitherman. Dir. USA: Walt Disney Pictures.

MORE FROM BRIGHTSUMMARIES.COM

- Reading guide – *Just So Stories* by Rudyard Kipling.
- Reading guide – *Kim* by Rudyard Kipling.

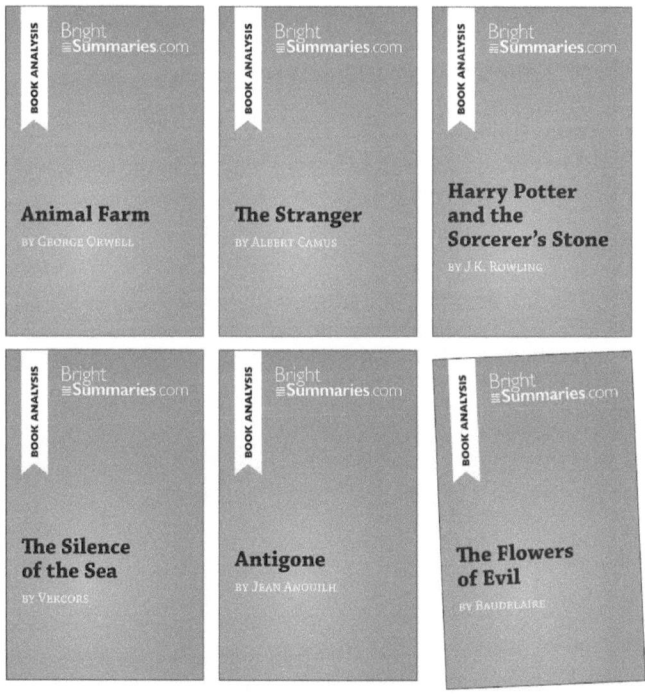

www.brightsummaries.com

Ebook EAN: 9782808017381

Paperback EAN: 9782808017398

Legal Deposit: D/2019/12603/36

Cover: © Primento

Digital conception by Primento, the digital partner of publishers.